Kriegsmarine Illustrated Ship Histories:

Pocket Battleship *Deutschland (Lutzow)*

By Antonio Bonomi
Illustrations by Abram Joslin
Nimble Books LLC

NIMBLE BOOKS LLC

ISBN-13: 978-1-934840-69-6
ISBN-10: 1-934840-69-6
Text © 2009 Antonio Bonomi
Illustrations © 2007, 2009 Abram Joslin.
Photographs from the collection of Antonio Bonomi.

Version 1.0; last saved 2009-07-07.

Nimble Books LLC
1521 Martha Avenue
Ann Arbor, MI 48103-5333
http://www.nimblebooks.com

The cover font, heading fonts and the body text inside the book are in Constantia, designed by John Hudson for Microsoft.

∞ The paper used in this publication meets the minimum requirements of the American National Standard for Information Sciences—Permanence of Paper for Printed Library Materials, ANSI Z39.48-1992. The paper is acid-free and lignin-free.

Contents

About the Author iv
Acknowledgements iv
The *Panzerschiffe Deutschland* 5
The *Schwere Kreuzer Lutzow* 20

ABOUT THE AUTHOR

Antonio Bonomi was born on 1960 in Italy. Currently he works for a major International computer company as a financial control manager. In the past he as been one of the engineers and new products manager for the same company on new computer design. He is married with two daughters and since he was 12 years old he started his own study of *Kriegsmarine* warships, his real passion and hobby. In recent years, taking advantage of the growth of the Internet, Antonio has released his own research through various websites and cooperated with the most advanced ones. His detailed research on the famous battle between *Hood* and *Bismarck* in the Denmark Strait is currently the reference of that historical event and was published in *Storia Militare* in Italy in December 2005. Antonio has produced the best current information about the technical evolution and camouflage schemes of the major *Kriegsmarine* warships of World War II.

ACKNOWLEDGEMENTS

I would like to thank some friends for the support in my research: Abram Joslin from USA, Philippe Caresse from France, Even Blomqvist from Norway, Kurt Johansen from Norway, Robert Gehringer from Germany, Markus Titsch from Germany, and Olaf Held from Germany.

THE *PANZERSCHIFFE DEUTSCHLAND*

Panzerschiffe A (Ersatz Preussen) was started at Deutsche Werke in Kiel on February 5, 1929, and launched on May 19, 1931, in the presence of the Weimar Republic President Von Hindenburg and the first Chancellor, Adolf Hitler. She was named *Deutschland*.

The *Deutschland* was the first high seas unit of the new born Weimar Republic *Marine*. The modern design of this ship, defined as a *Panzerschiffe* (armoured ship), was a result of the limits imposed on Germany after the end of World War One. Within the 10.000-tons treaty limit, the German designers successfully assembled, all the characteristics needed by a good high seas raider. . She had electrically soldered hull plates, two triple 280-mm main gun turrets, and diesel engines, insuring good speed and long range autonomy. She was surely superior to the heavy cruisers of any potential enemies and faster than any heavy battleship of the Royal Navy, her most likely adversary. This left *HMS Hood, Renown* and *Repulse* as the only Royal Navy units that both were capable of catching this fast ship and had superior broadsides.

During 1934, 1935 and 1936 she was modified with a new mast, rangefinders, cranes and platforms on the upper works and secondary armament. In the same period she went on various cruises to European harbors (Norway, Mediterranean Sea, Baltic). At every stop, experts of all navies were very curious to come and see the innovative "Pocket Battleship."

Deutschland participated as an "international control unit" during the Spanish Civil War, in 1936, 1937 and 1938. German warships could be easily recognized because of the national colours large stripes painted horizontally on their main turrets (black, white and red). Naples was chosen as a Mediterranean Sea base.

Deutschland was with her sister ship *Admiral Scheer* anchored at Ibiza Island when, on the morning of May 29, 1937, she was bombed by some Spanish Repubican airplanes. The result of this international incident was tragic: 31 dead and 78 wounded. As a response to the Republicans, Berlin ordered *Admiral Scheer* to bombard the city of Almeria on May 31, 1937. *Deutschland* returned to Germany at Deutsche Werke in Kiel where she was repaired.

Figure 1. The launch of the Panzerschiffe *Deutschland* on May 19, 1931 at Deutsche Werke in Kiel. On that day, the German *Marine* was reborn, after the sad end of the Kaiserliche High Seas fleet at Scapa Flow in the aftermath of World War One. The ship was completed in two years and was finally commissioned on April 1, 1933 as the Weimar Republic Marine fleet flagship based in Wilhelmshaven.

PANZERSCHIFFE DEUTSCHLAND (LUTZOW)

Figure 2. Above, the Weimar Republic Marine flag; below, the coat of arm of Panzerschiffe *Deutschland* visible in peace time on both sides of the warship bow.

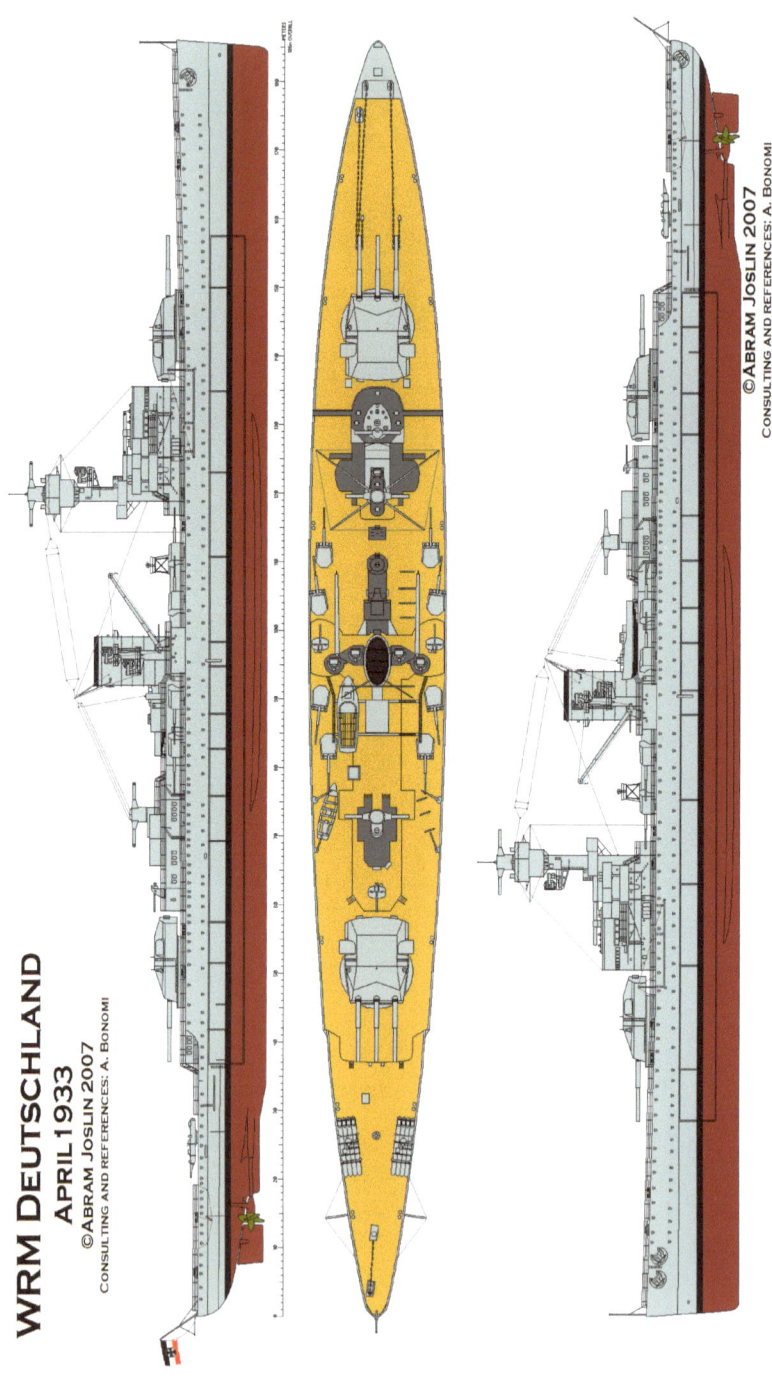

Figure 3. Profiles and plan, April 1933. (illustration by Abram Joslin)

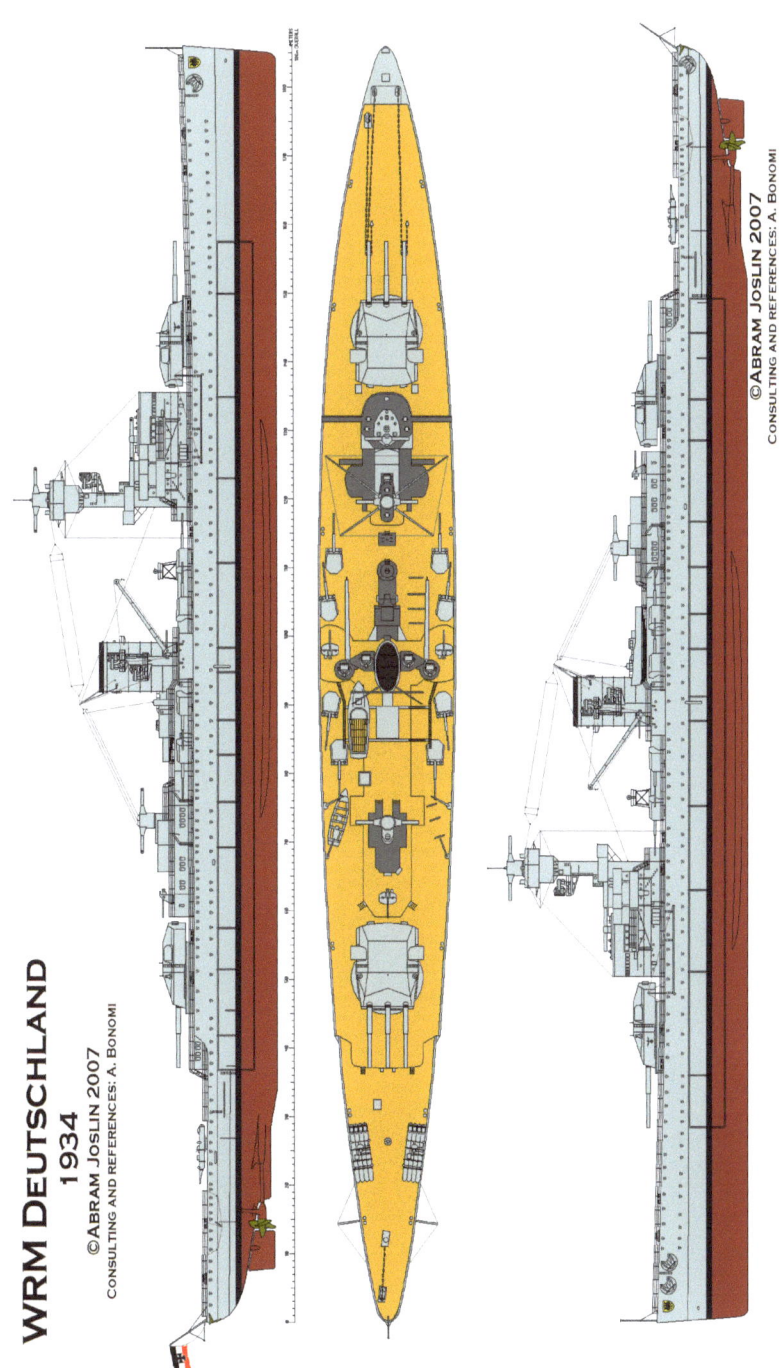

Figure 4. Profiles and plan, 1934. (Illustration by Abram Joslin)

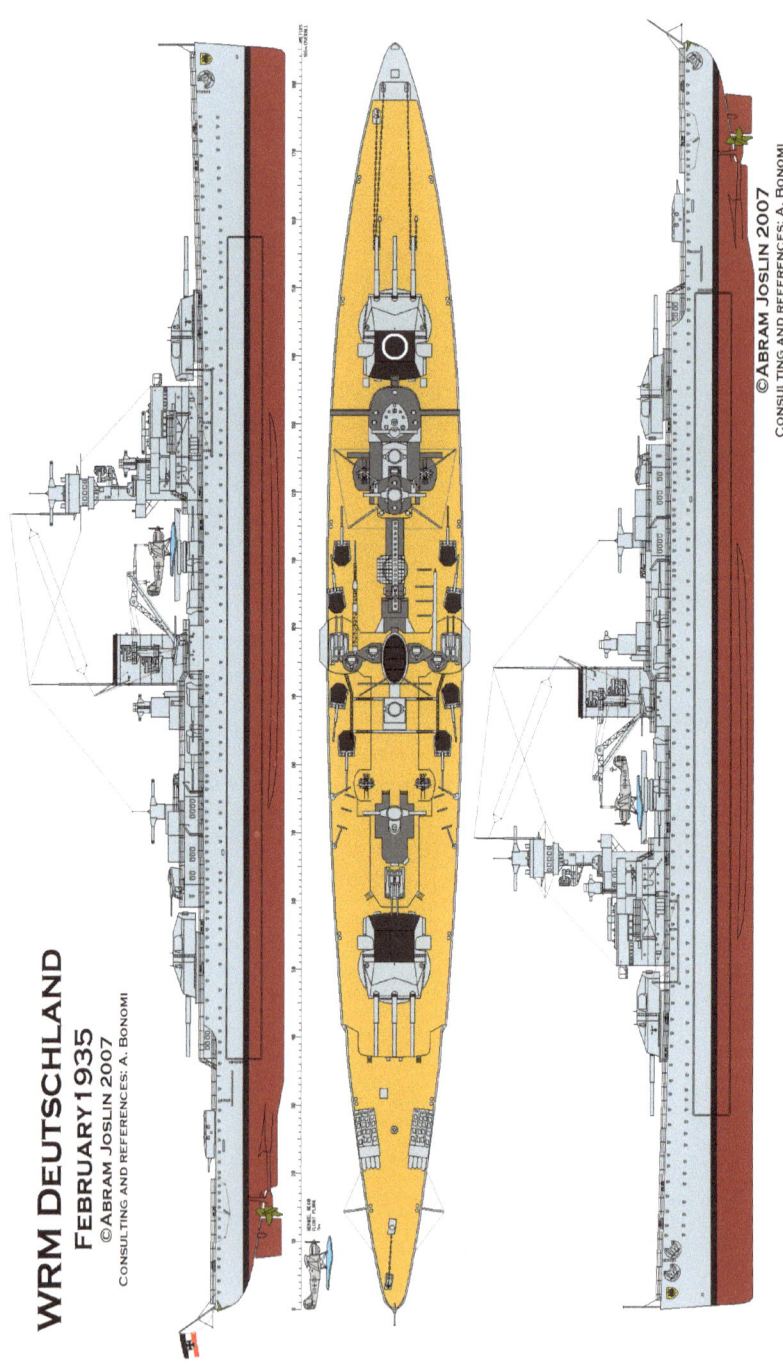

Figure 5. Profiles and plan, February 1935. (Illustration by Abram Joslin)

Figure 6. On November 7, 1935 the Weimar Republic Marine flag was replaced with the new *Kriegsmarine* war flag.

Figure 7. *Panzerschiffe Deutschland in* 1935, notice the Weimar Republic flags.

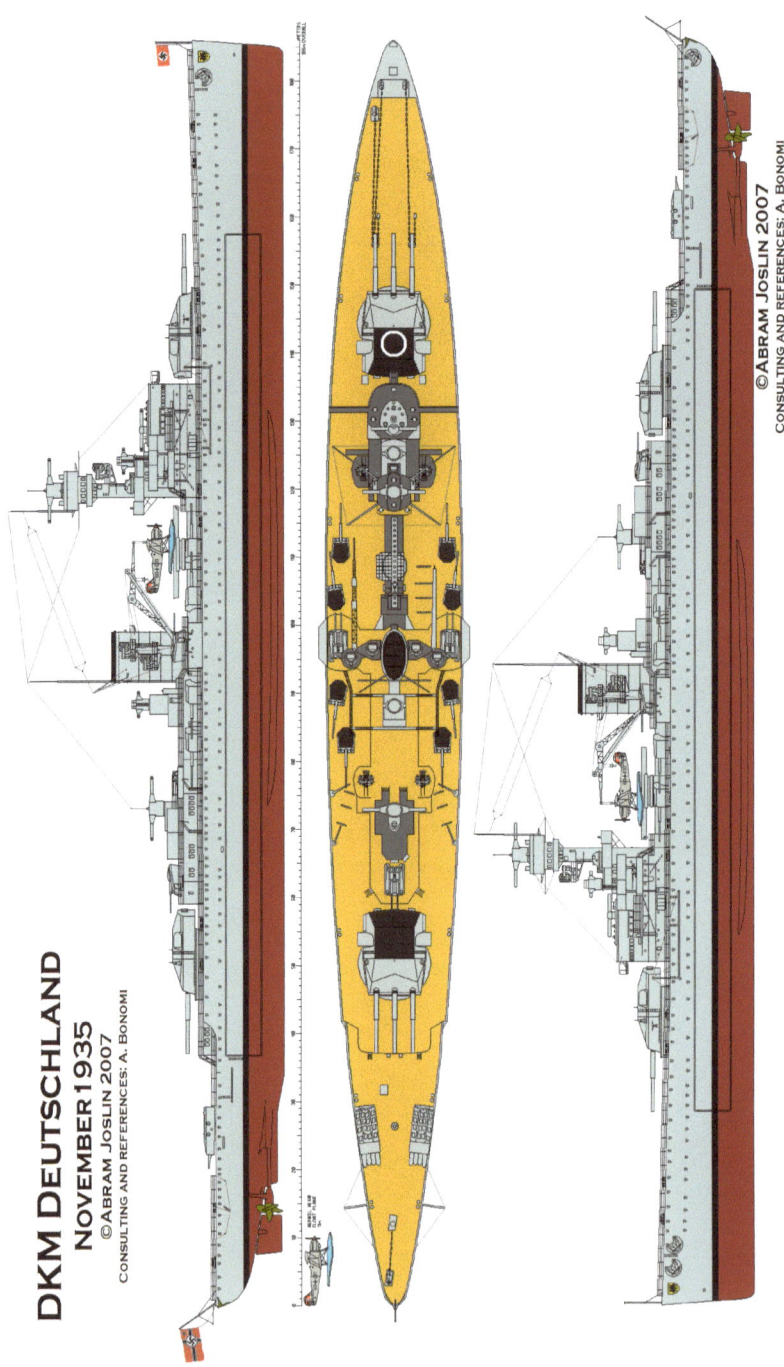

Figure 8. Profiles and plan, November 1935. (Illustrations by Abram Joslin)

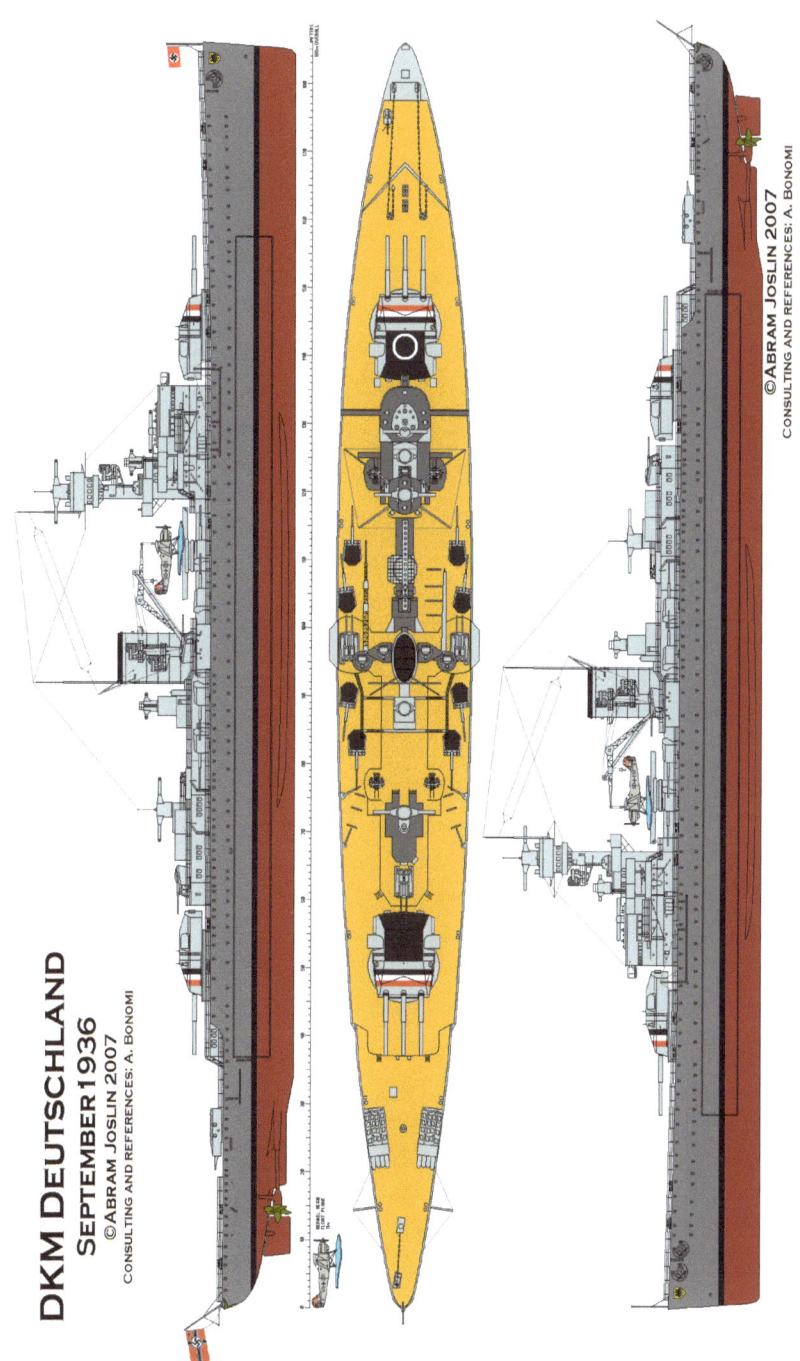

Figure 9. Profiles and plan, September 1936. (Illustration by Abram Joslin)

Figure 10. *Panzerschiffe Deutschland* in 1936 during Spain war time; in the background *Admiral Scheer*.

PANZERSCHIFFE DEUTSCHLAND (LUTZOW)

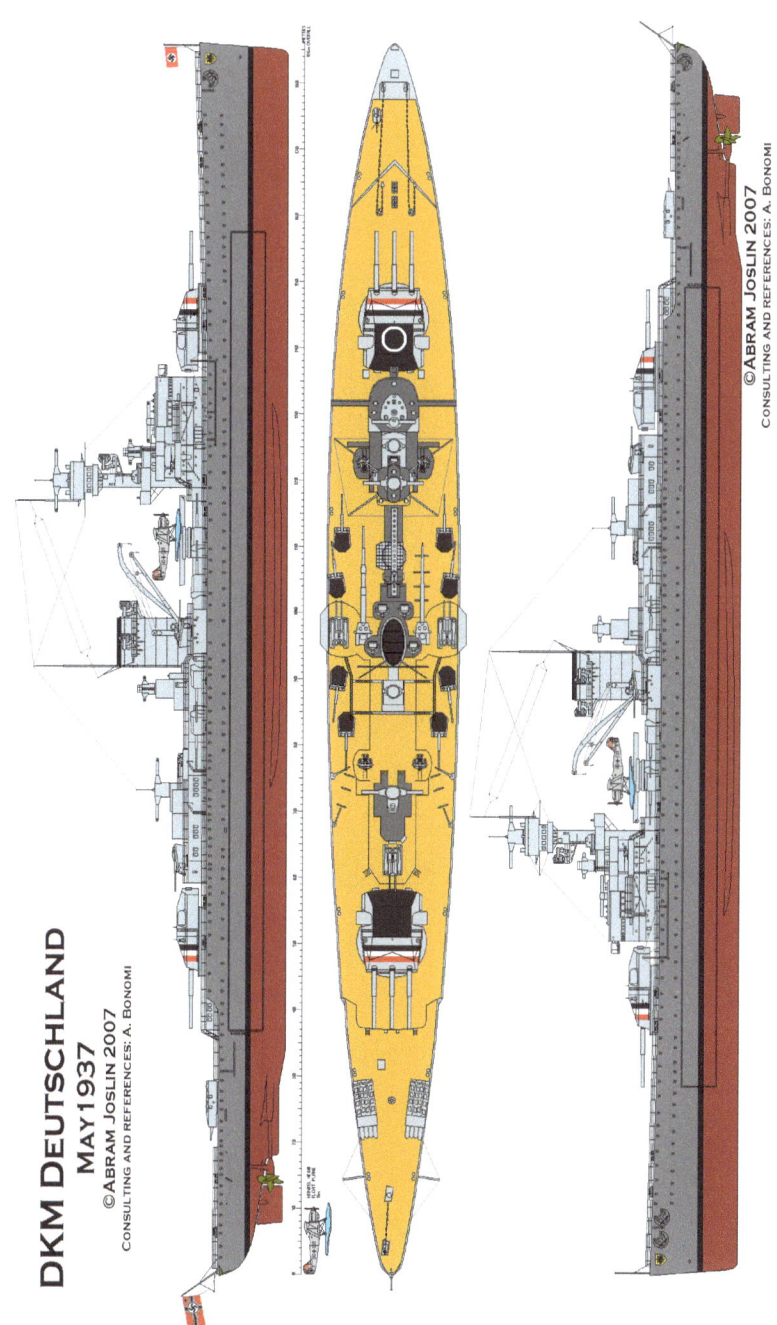

Figure 11. Profiles and plan, May 1937. (Illustration by Abram Joslin)

In 1938 and 1939 there were other works and weapons updates, with the old biplane Heinkel 60 replaced by the new Arado 196 and the addition of the FuMo 23/39 radar on the mainmast.

In May 1939, a German fleet squadron composed of the three *Panzerschiffe*—*Deutschland, Admiral Scheer* and *Admiral Graf Spee*—plus the light cruisers *Leipzig, Koln* and *Nurnberg,* escorted by the destroyers *Leeberecht Maas (Z1), Richard Beitzen (Z4), Georg Thiele (Z2), Max Schulz (Z3), Friedrich Ihn (Z14), Friedrich Eckholdt (Z16)* and *Hermann Kunne (Z19)* sailed from German bases to occupy the Memel peninsula in Lituania. On board *Deutschland* was the Fuhrer, Adolf Hitler, with the *Kriegsmarine* High Command. The squadron did not meet any resistance from enemy forces.

As war began, *Deutschland* sailed through the Denmark Strait into the Atlantic Ocean and remained in the northern part of it, sinking two ships, the British *Stonegate* and the Norwegian *L. W. Hansen,* and capturing the American *City of Flint,* which was carrying weapons for England. The capture of this neutral ship caused an international incident that, together with some diesel engines problems, made SKL call *Deutschland* back home; the warship reached Gotenhafen on November 15, 1939.

The international incident with the *City of Flint,* in which the name *Deutschland* figured unfavourably in international news, was the main reason for the ship's name to be changed from *Deutschland* to *Lutzow* on November 16, 1939, as recorded in the ship's log book—but only officially announced by *Ober Kommando Marine* (OKM) on January 25, 1940.

Sailors are very superstitious and a ship having a name changed is supposed to make it unlucky. The future war years showed that the crew of *Lutzow* had something to think about.

PANZERSCHIFFE DEUTSCHLAND (LUTZOW)

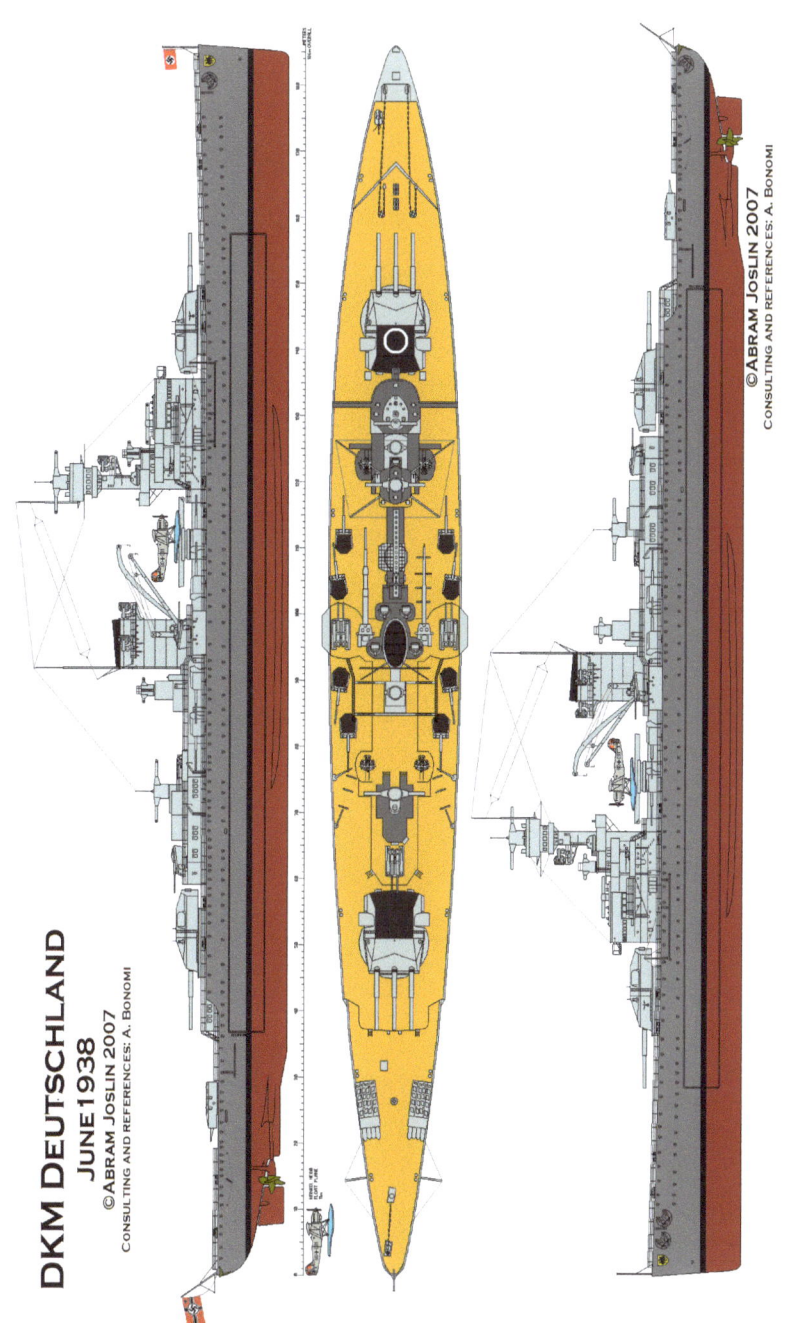

Figure 12. Profiles and plan, June 1938. (Illustration by Abram Joslin)

Figure 13. Early 1939; notice coat of arms on the bow, the air recognition marks on the top main turrets and the small funnel cap that has been added.

PANZERSCHIFFE DEUTSCHLAND (LUTZOW)

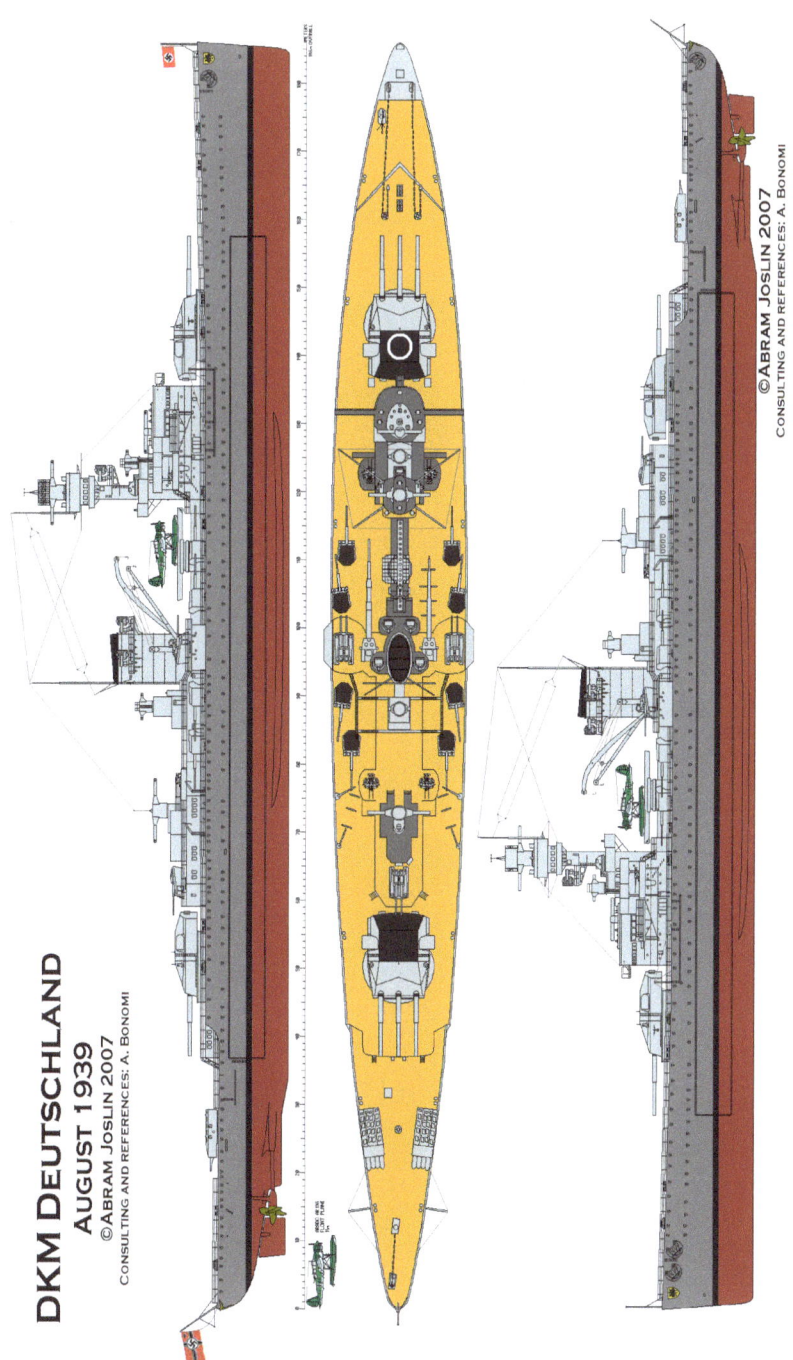

Figure 14. Profiles and plan, August 1939. (Illustration by Abram Joslin)

The Schwere Kreuzer Lutzow

The *Lutzow* remained in the Baltic Sea for some tactical missions before being put into Danzig yard for an engine refit that lasted until February 1940.

Spring of 1940 was coming and after various incidents involving Norway, the German High Command, decided on the Norwegian invasion, code named Operation *Weserübung,* in April 1940.

Lutzow was attached to Group 5: destination, Oslo. The group was under the command of Vice-Admiral Oscar Kummetz with his flag on the heavy cruiser *Blücher*. The group also included the light cruiser *Emden* and the torpedo boats *Mowe, Kondor and Albatros* plus the minesweepers *R-17* and *R-24*.

On the morning of April 8, 1940, the group entered the Oslo fjord, immediately finding strong resistance by the Norwegians. In the middle of

Figure 15. *Lutzow*'s seal.

Oslo fjord is the Drøbak strait, where the Oskarsborg fortress was located. From the fortress four 280-mm guns fired at *Blücher,* which was sunk later by shore-based torpedoes; the same guns hit the *Lutzow* on her A-ANTON turret, destroying the center 280 mm gun, and the group was forced to withdraw.

Nevertheless, within 36 hours, the city of Oslo fell into German hands and the group could enter the Norwegian capital harbour where *Lutzow* anchored.

On April 11, 1940, while coming back from Oslo, the *Lutzow* was torpedoed on the stern by the British submarine *HMS Spearfish*. Damage was extensive and the warship almost lost her entire stern section. She took 1300 tons of water onboard. She was towed and escorted arriving in Kiel at Deutsche Werke on April 14 on late evening. One year's work was needed to replace the entire after section of the ship.

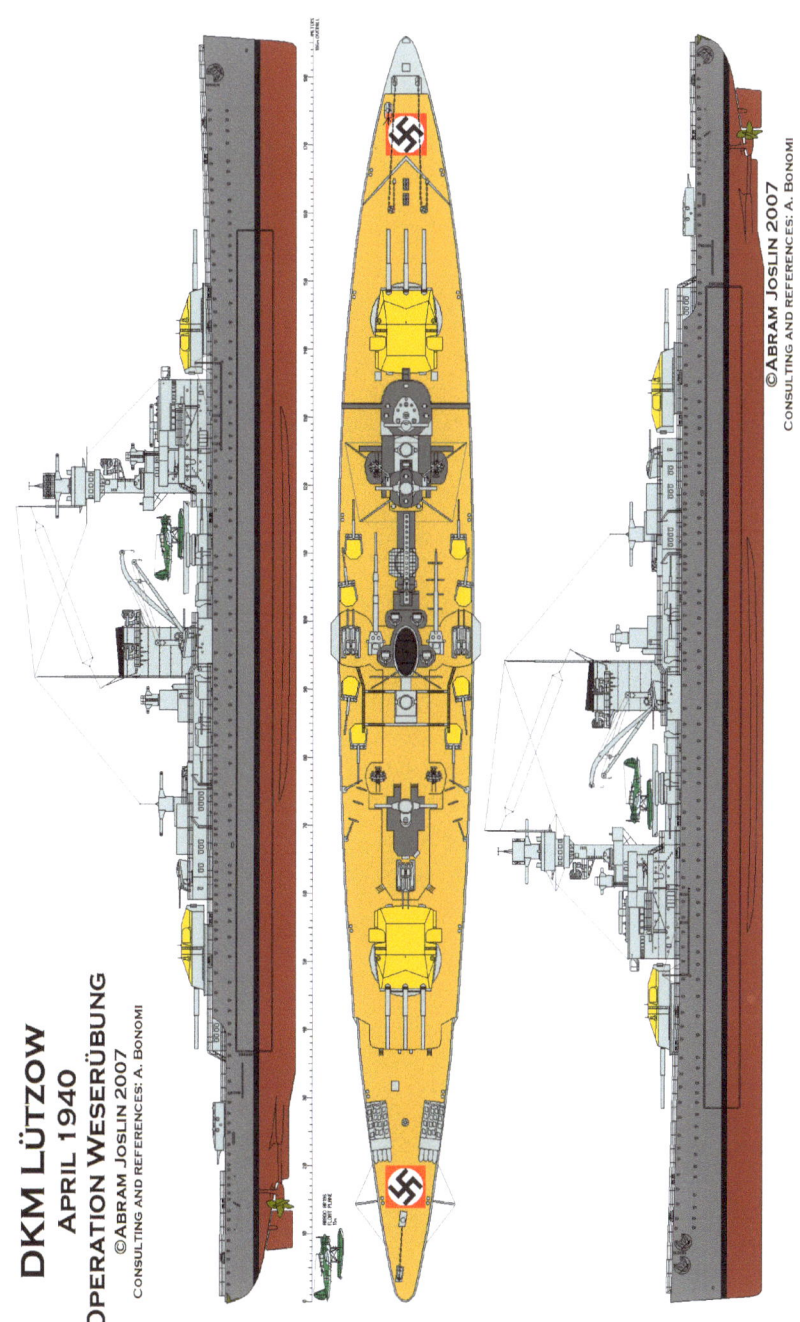

Figure 16. Profiles and plans of *Lutzow* in April 1940, at the time of Operation Weserübung. (Illustration by Abram Joslin)

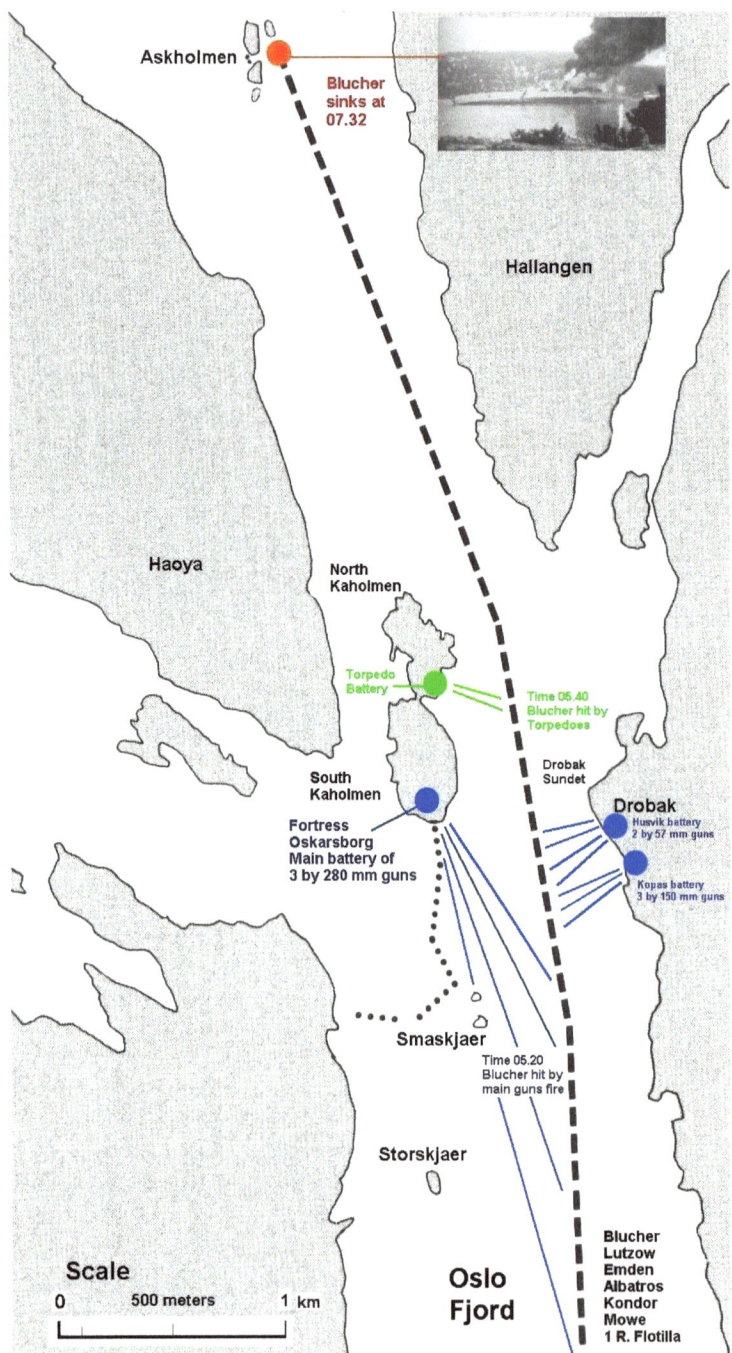

Figure 17. Map of Oslo Fjord entrance with the Oskarsborg fortress and Drøback strait.

Figure 18. *Lutzow* enters Oslo Fjord on April 10, 1940.

Figure 19. April 1940, *Lutzow* torpedoed by *HMS Spearfish* slowly sails back to Kiel. Notice the stern deep on the water and the missing central gun on the triple A-Anton turret.

Lutzow was re-commissioned on March 31, 1941 and started training on April and May ready for a new Atlantic cruise.

The loss of battleship *Bismarck* in May 1941 changed the *Kriegsmarine's* priorities and *Lutzow* was ordered to sail to Norway.

The ship sailed on June 11, 1941 for Trondheim executing Operation *Sommereise*, escorted by 5 destroyers.

While sailing north between Lindesnes and Egersund in the vicinity of Karmoy she was torpedoed by a RAF torpedo bomber (a Bristol Beaufort flown by Sergeant Loveitt) which inflicted a torpedo hit at midships on the port side, making a huge hole on the hull. Other airplanes tried to attack the damaged ship unsuccessfully.

The heavily damaged warship, listing 21 degrees and with only one one shaft operational, sailed back at 16 knots for Kiel at Deutsche Werke where she arrived on June 14, 1941 entering dock VI.

Necessary repair works were estimated as requiring 6 months.

PANZERSCHIFFE DEUTSCHLAND (LÜTZOW)

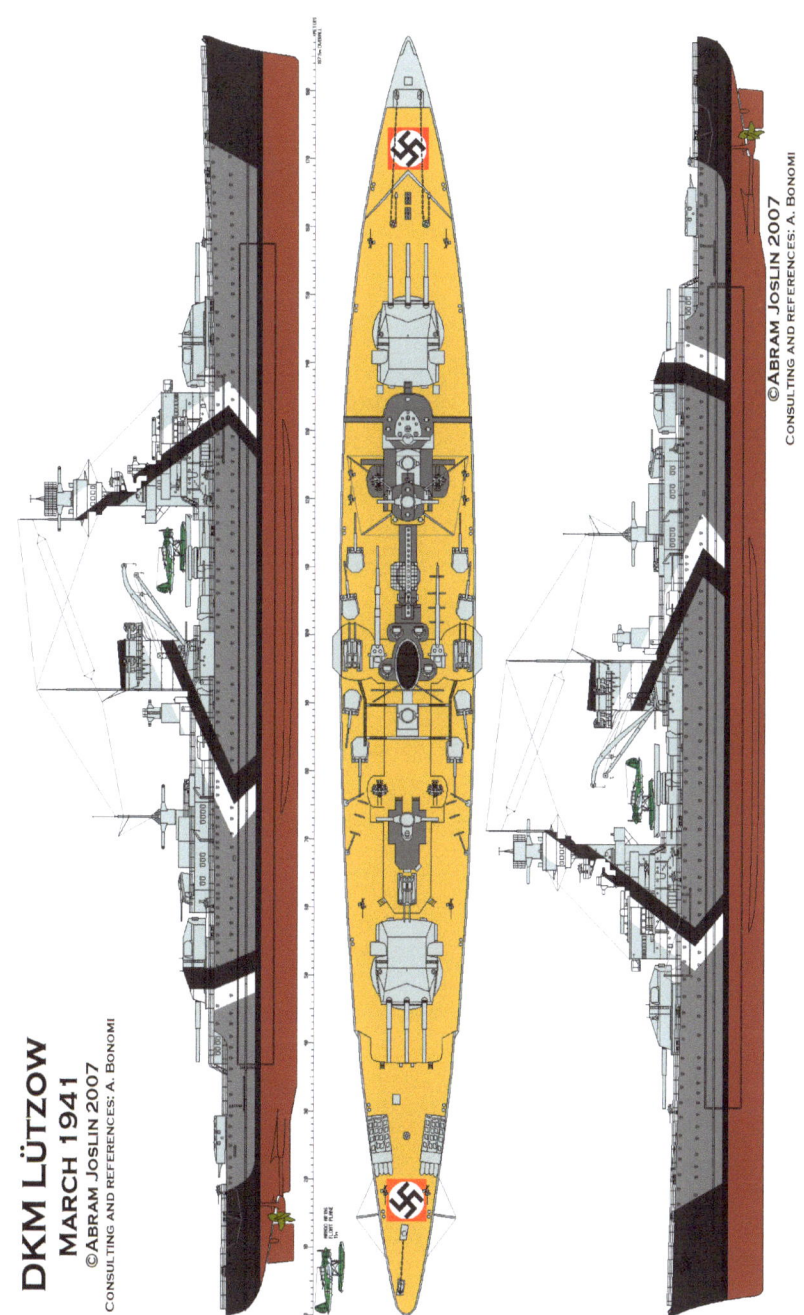

Figure 20. Profiles and plans of *Lutzow* repaired, March 1941. (Illustration by Abram Joslin)

Figure 21. *Lutzow* in Gotenhafen on April 12, 1941; in the background *Bismarck*.

Figure 22. *Lutzow* in late April 1941 anchored in Danzig bay; notice the new radar on top of the main tower.

Figure 23. *Lutzow* with dark grey torpedo tubes in early june 1941 ready for Operation *Sommereise*.

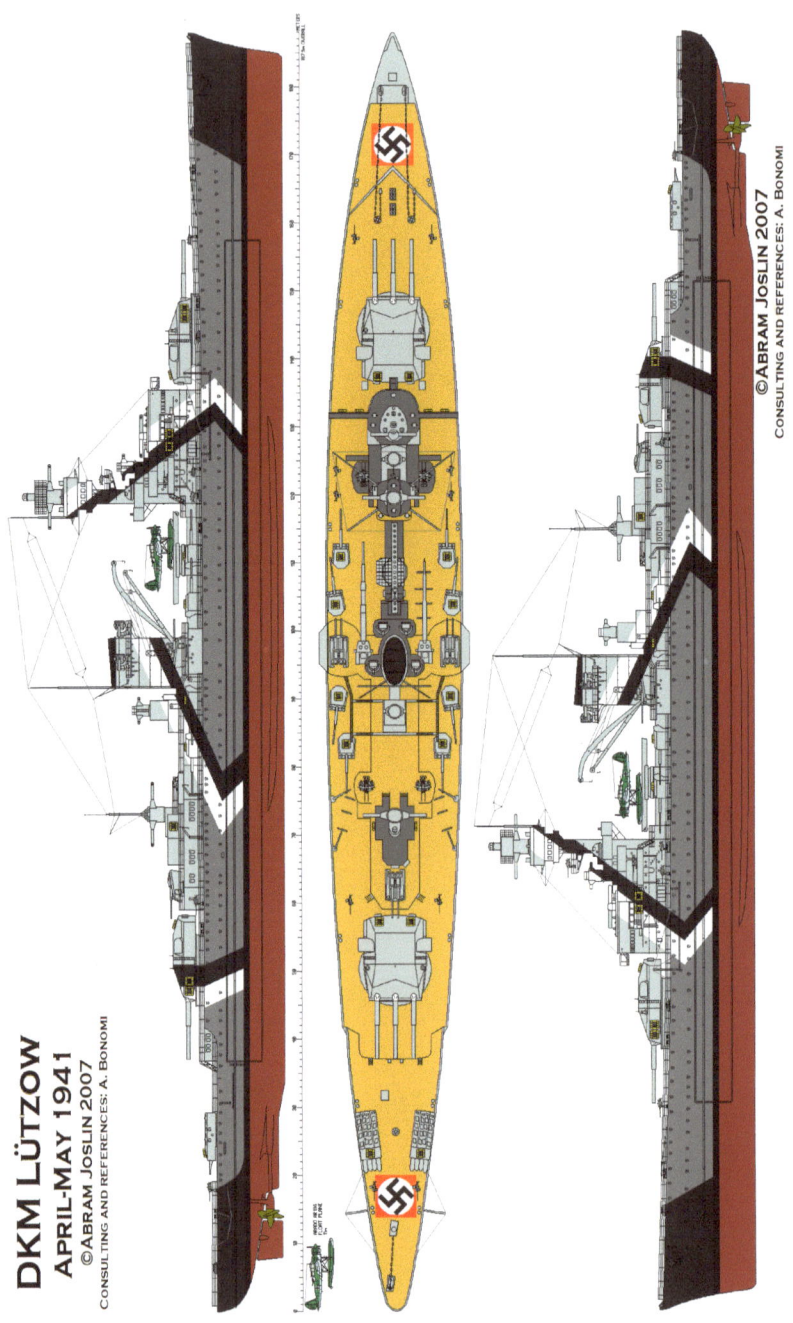

Figure 24. Profiles and plan, April/May 1941.(Illustration by Abram Joslin)

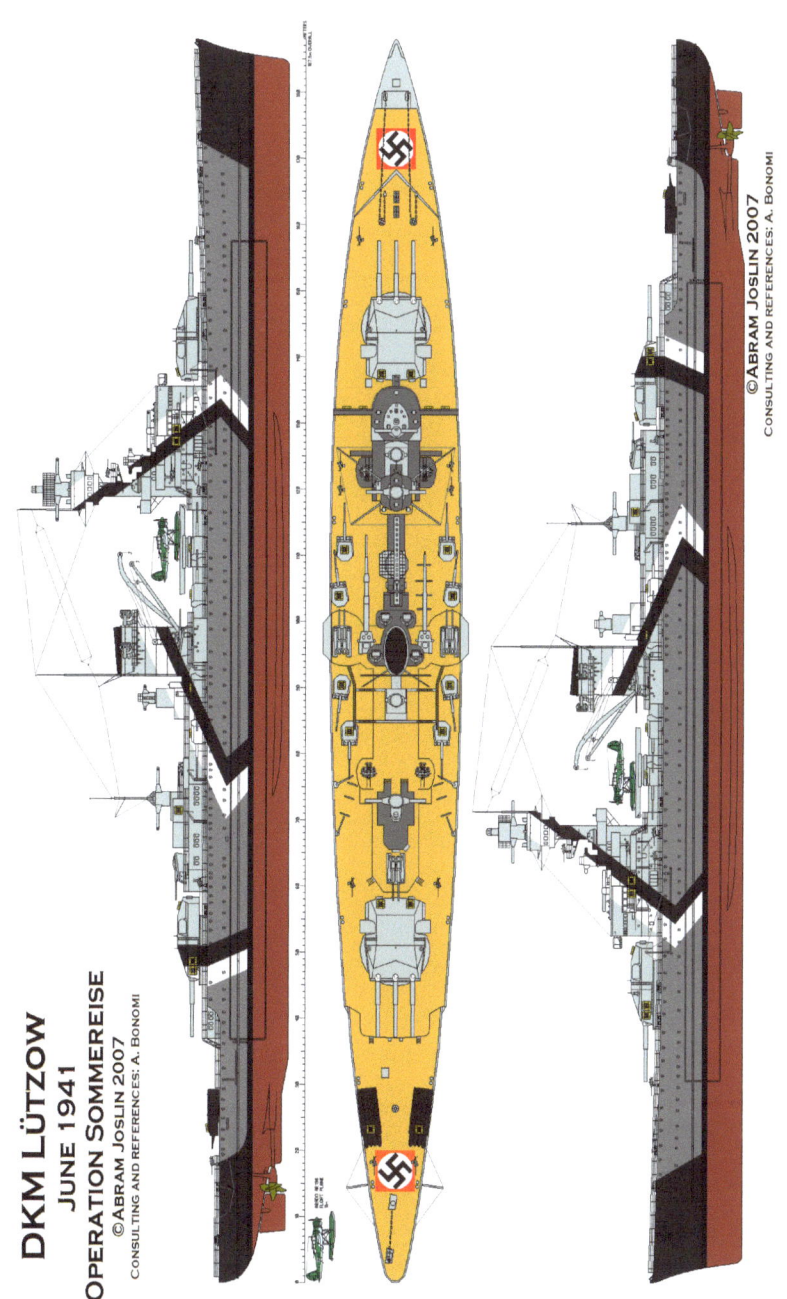

Figure 25. Profiles and plan, June 1941. (Illustration by Abram Joslin)

The repairs were completed by early 1942, when *Lutzow* emerged again from the dockyard and sailed to Gotenhafen on January 17, starting a new re-training period.

It was only on May 15, 1942 that *Lutzow*, escorted by four destroyers, started Operation *Waltzertraum* and sailed from Swinemunde thru Kiel and then to Norway. After a stop into KvarenesFjord, Kristansand, she anchored successfully and undamaged into LoFjord,-Trondheim on May 19, 1942.

But *Lutzow* was supposed to operate jointly with her sister ship *Admiral Scheer* out of Narvik. Consequently on May 24, 1942 she sailed north with three destroyers and the tanker *Nordmark,* arriving at Bogen Bay on May 25 and anchoring aside the *Admiral Scheer.*

Lutzow did some training with *Admiral Scheer* and a destroyer flotilla in June 1942, and then began operating together out of Narvik.

The first occasion was Operation *Rosselsprung* on early July 1942 against allied convoy PQ 17. There were two groups to be used on this operation, one out of Trondheim with *Tirpitz* and *Admiral Hipper* escorted by five destroyers and the second one from Narvik composed of *Lutzow* and *Admiral Scheer* escorted by six destroyers.

On July 2, 1942 the order was given to move from their anchorages and join into AltaFjord ready to start the attack against the allied convoy in Arctic waters.

As she sailed out of Narvik's-OfotFjord through the Tjelsundet strait, the *Lutzow* ran aground and seriously damaged some compartments. The warship was called back into the starting anchorage at Bogen Bay and the damage was inspected.

Despite *Lutzow*'s inglorious role in the sortie, the mere presence of the *Kriegsmarine* warships, including the *Tirpitz*, frightened the Royal Navy into scattering the PQ 17 convoy. All its merchant ships were sunk by *U-Boote* and *Luftwaffe* airplanes.

To be repaired, *Lutzow* needed to sail back to Germany; *Lutzow* was initially moved south into LoFjord-Trondheim and, on August 10, 1942, in an operation codenamed *Hermelin*, she sailed back to Germany, reaching Deutsche Werke at Kiel on August 12, 1942.

Figure 26. *Lutzow* wearing the dark grey camo scheme in spring 1942.

Figure 27. Operation *Waltzertraum*, *Lutzow* escorted by destroyers successfully on her way to Norway in May 1942.

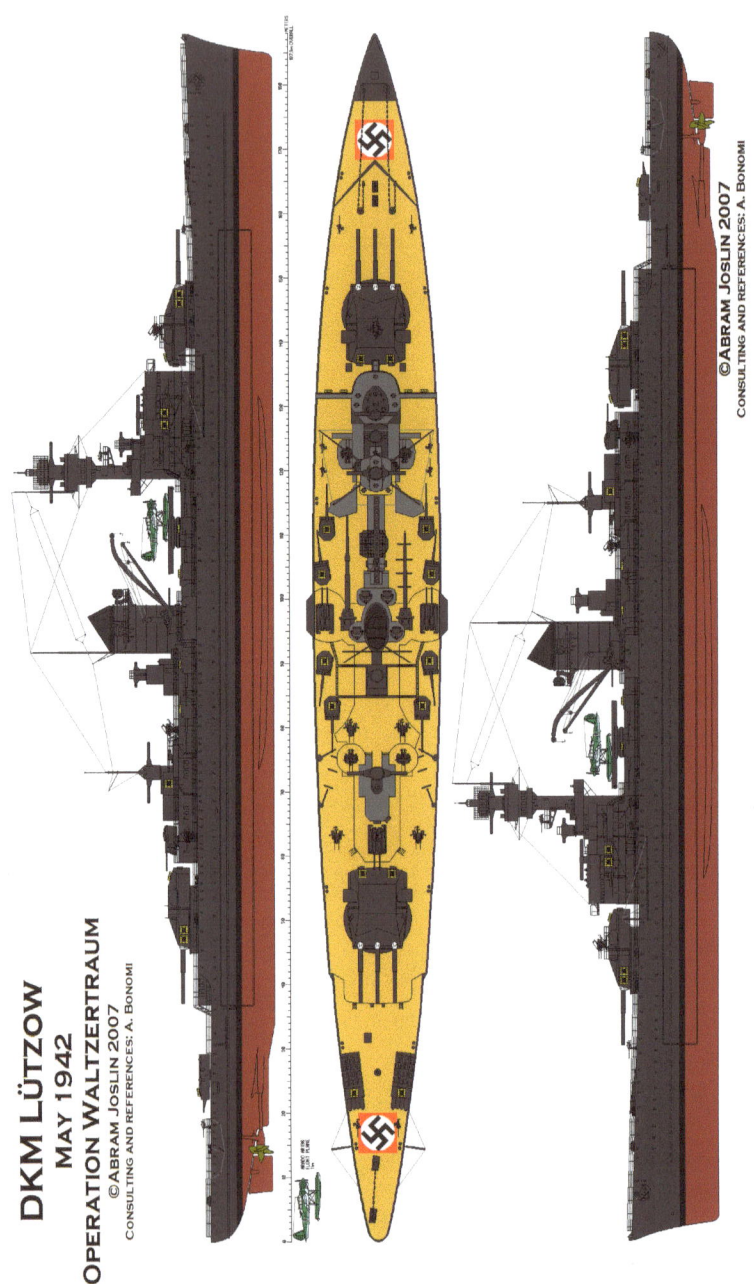

Figure 28. *Lutzow* in May 1942 in full dark grey dress for Operation *Waltzertraum* and her final successful transfer to Norway. Notice the 5 A/A 20 mm *flakvierling* added; one on top of Anton turret and four on the after platforms, plus a new added radar set.

PANZERSCHIFFE DEUTSCHLAND (LUTZOW)

Figure 29. *Lutzow*, still in dark grey camo, followed by *Admiral Scheer* and some destroyers on trials into OfotFjord on June 1942.

Figure 30. *Lutzow* is anchored in Bogen bay on July 1942 after the damage on the hull on Tjelsundet.

NIMBLE BOOKS LLC

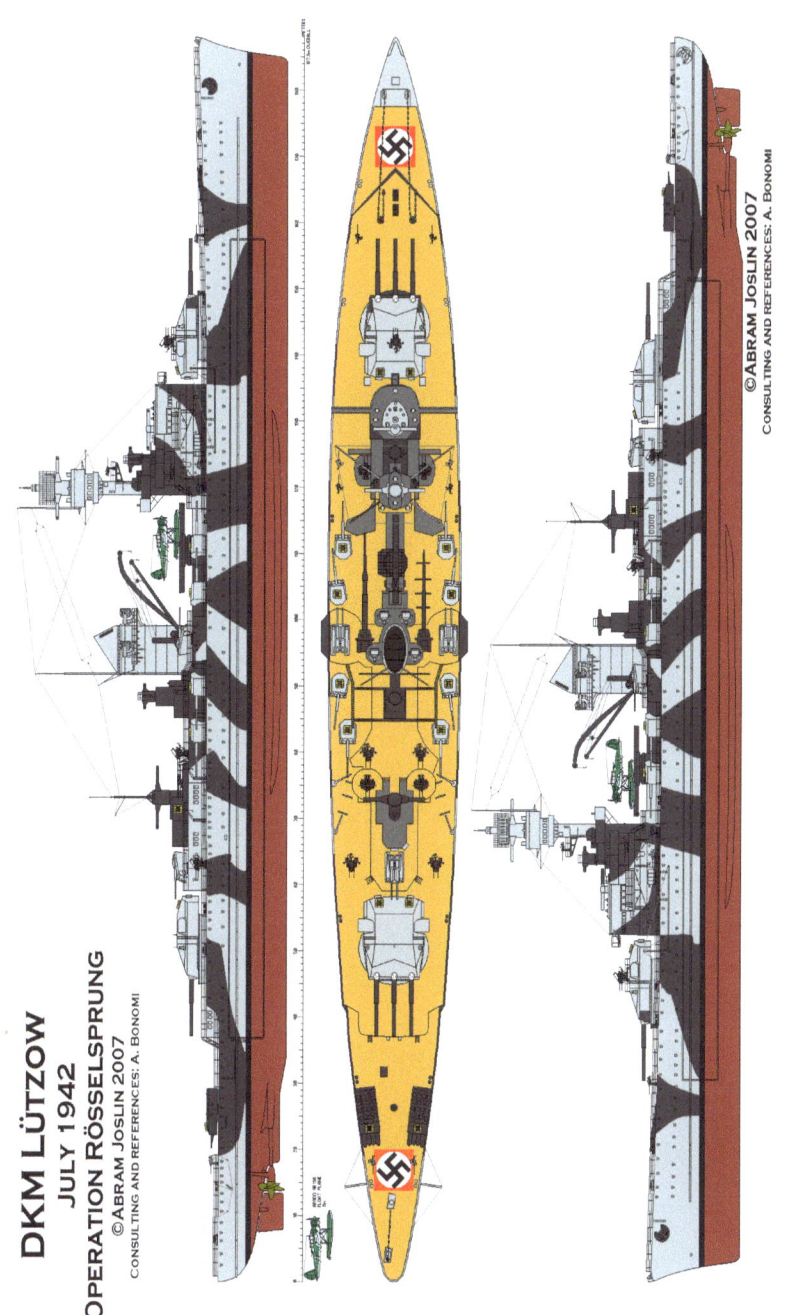

Figure 31. Lützow at the time of Operational Rösselsprung (July 1942). Illustration by Abram Joslin

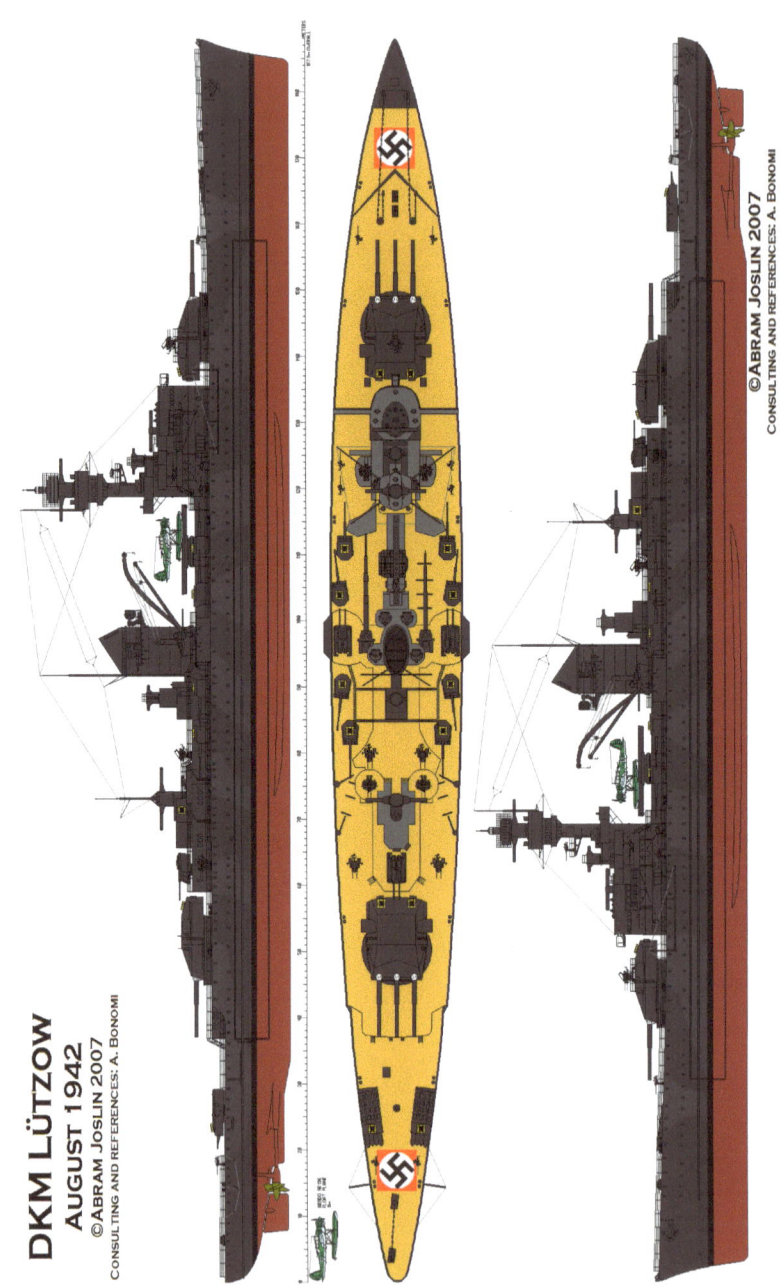

Figure 32. Profiles and plans for *Lutzow* in early August 1942, with dark camo on top of Operation*Rossselsprung* camo, ready to sail back to Germany. (Illustration by Abram Joslin)

Figure 33. *Lutzow* anchored inside anti-torpedo nets at LoFjord at Trondheim in early August 1942.

Repair work ended on November 1942 and, after the usual trials on the Baltic Sea, *Lutzow* began Operation *Prometheus*. She sailed back to Norway on December 10, 1942, escorted by the three destroyers *Z-6 Theodor Riedel, Z-20 Karl Galster* and *Z-31*, arriving in Narvik into Bogen bay on December 12, 1942.

On December 17, 1942, *Lutzow* sailed north executing Operation *Rudelsburg* and reached AltaFjord into KaaFjord where she met the cruisers *Admiral Hipper, Nurnberg* and *Koln*.

After the PQ 17 convoy disaster, the Allied changed their strategy and instead of a big convoy heavily protected from the air, they broke it into smaller convoys with local light warship protection against *U-Boote* and heavy warships force coverage in the area, so that the Royal Navy's heavy ships could protect both convoys. JW 51 was divided as said into JW 51-A and JW 51-B and sailed from Loch Ewe on December 15, 1942.

On December 30, 1942, Vice-Admiral Oscar Kummetz took out from AltaFjord the heavy cruiser *Admiral Hipper* and *Lutzow* escorted by six destroyers in Operation *Regenbogen*, the attack to convoy JW 51.

The result was probably the most embarrassing defeat *Kriegsmarine* heavy units had to suffer during World War II while at sea.

The German warships met initially the very light group of five destroyers *HMS Onslow, Obedient, Obdurate, Orwell* and *Achates* covering the convoy plus later the two light cruisers *HMS Sheffield* and *HMS Jamaica* that were escorted by another two destroyers.

The superior German units never reached the convoy merchant ships that were their real target. In addition they lost the destroyer *Z-16 Friedrich Eckholdt* and suffered various damage to the heavy ships, while the Royal Navy lost the destroyer *Achates* and the minesweeper *Bramble* and endured heavy damages to the other heroic destroyers.

The result of the Battle on the Barents Sea should have been far superior for the *Kriegsmarine*. Once Hitler was informed of the results, he became furious and removed Admiral Erich Raeder from his *Gross-Admiral* position, promoting Admiral Karl Donitz on his place. Immediately many heavy warships were decommissioned and all new units were suspended or cancelled. This was basically the end of German heavy surface activity during second world war.

Figure 34. *Lutzow* on trials, ready to sail back to Norway, in early December 1942.

Figure 35. *Lutzow* anchored in Barbrudalen enclosure inside KaaFjord, in December 1942, ready for Operation *Regenbogen*.

Lutzow was not involved in the initial decommissioning of *Kriegsmarine* heavy warships because Admiral Donitz convinced the Fuhrer Adolf Hitler that some German warships were needed to threaten the Allied convoys on the arctic waters.

For this reason *Scharnhorst* was sent to Norway, reaching Narvik on March 1943, *Tirpitz* was moved north as well and the two battleships joined *Lutzow* in Narvik. After some trials, they went up north anchoring in the new *Kriegsmarine* permanent base established into AltaFjord on the KaaFjord.

The concentration of so many German warships forced the Allies to stop the Arctic convoys and wait for winter to allow better chances to pass without being attacked.

For this reason *Lutzow's only* activity during this period was in August 1943 when she sailed toward Novaja Zemlia, executing Operation *Husar.* No enemy ships were seen by the *Luftwaffe,* so after a week the operation was cancelled.

Meanwhile, the Royal Navy was not sleeping, and on September 1943 they sent midget submarines—the famous X-Craft—to attack the German warships in the KaaFjord. The main target was of course the *Tirpitz,* but *Scharnhorst* and *Lutzow* were also initially considered by the attacking submarines.

The British attack was a success and *Tirpitz* was seriously damaged on September 22, but the loss of many X-Craft approaching KaaFjord forced the British to concentrate their attack only on *Tirpitz.*

Lutzow was on LangFjord for some repairs when the attack took place and immediately after, on September 23, it was decided to send her back to Germany, escorted by three destroyers, because the work needed was not possible in Norway.

The ships reached Kiel on September 29, 1943 and started a six month repair activity. *SKL* never made plans to send her back to Norway.

From October 1943 until June 1944, *Lutzow* was in the dockyards. After the execution of these major repairs, trials were carried out in the Gotenhafen area of the Baltic Sea.

In June 1944 *Lutzow* was ready again, and she was used together with *Admiral Scheer* and *Prinz Eugen,* plus a six- destroyer flotilla, as a ready to use intervention squadron: the "Group Thiele." Together with the " Group Rogge" they were used against the Red Army and to protect Germans escaping from Russian occupied areas in late 1944.

In late June 1944 *Lutzow* was modernized and equipped with additional anti-aircraft guns and radars.

Memel, Libau, Riga Gulf, Konigsberg, Elbing: the ships were helping wherever they could, but the situation on the Eastern Front was becoming really dramatic. Gotenhafen was evacuated in March 1945, and the battle cruiser *Gneisenau*'s hull was sunk to block the harbor entrance.

In April 1945 *Lutzow* and three destroyers helped 38.000 refugees escape from the Hela peninsula in Operation *Walpurgisnacht*.

Lutzow was in Swinemunde when on April 16, 1945 she was attacked by Royal Air Force Avro-Lancaster bombers arrmed with Tallboys bombs (5. 2 tons each); the same bombs had been used to sink the *Tirpitz* at Tromso.

She received three close hits and was beached to prevent her sinking (53°56' North / 14°17' west).

The ship could still be used as a floating battery covering a radius of 46.6 km with her 280 mm guns and 25.7 km with the 150 mm guns.

Lutzow fired on the Red Army as it advanced towards Stettin until it became clear that they were about to reach Swinemunde. At that point, with the war ending, the *Kriegsmarine* high command decided to prevent the remaining heavy ships from falling into Russian hands. Consequently *Lutzow* was scuttled by her own crew on May 4, 1945.

In 1947 the wreck of *Lutzow* was salvaged by the Russians and towed to Kaliningrad in Poland (formerly known as the German city of Konigsberg).

Lutzow was sunk in front of the current Polish city of Kolobrzeg (formerly, the German Pomeranian city of Kolberg) on August 22, 1947.

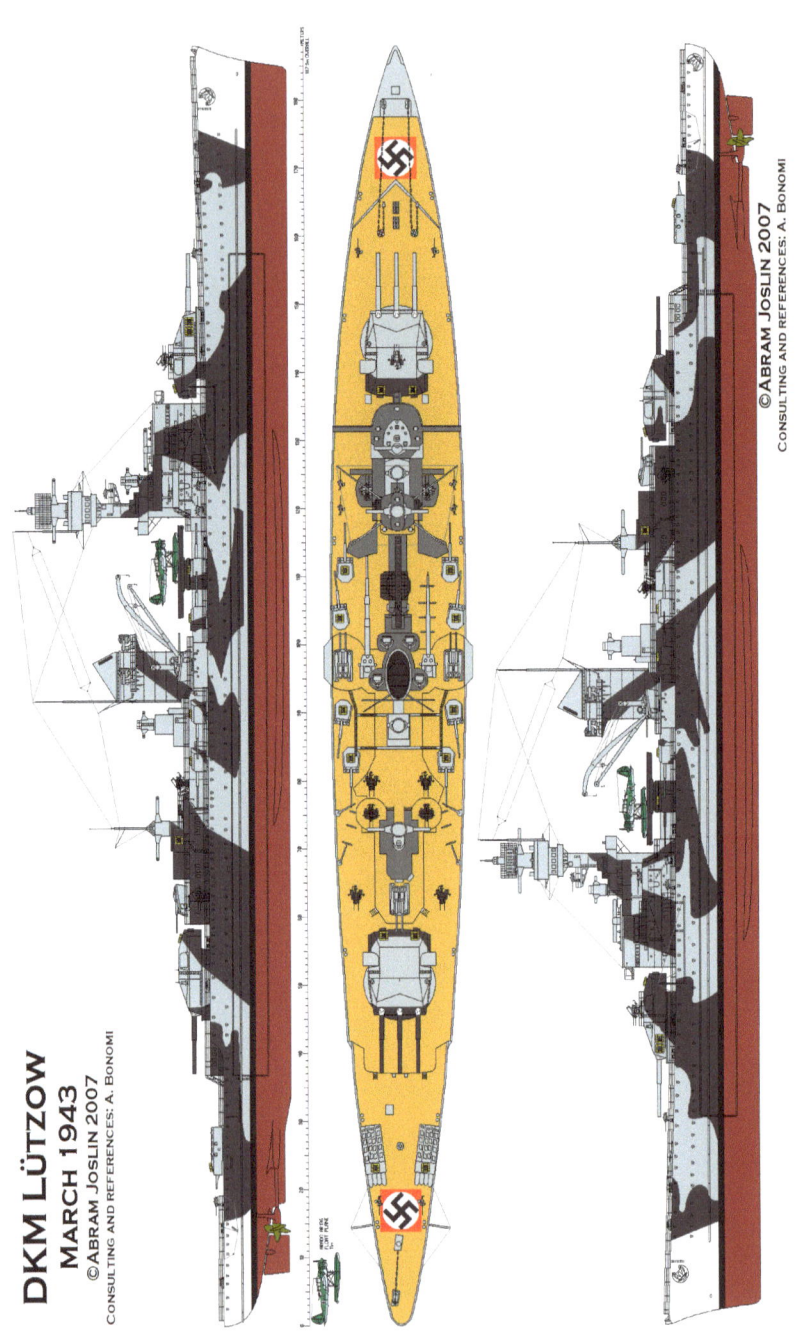

Figure 36. *Lutzow* in early 1943 in Norway with the new dazzle camouflage scheme.

PANZERSCHIFFE DEUTSCHLAND (LUTZOW)

Figure 37. *Lutzow* anchored in KaaFjord on early 1943; notice the new camouflage scheme and the double radar set on top main tower rangefinder, one on each side.

Figure 38. *Lutzow* anchored at LangFjord at Sopnes bay with the *Husar* camo scheme on August 1943.

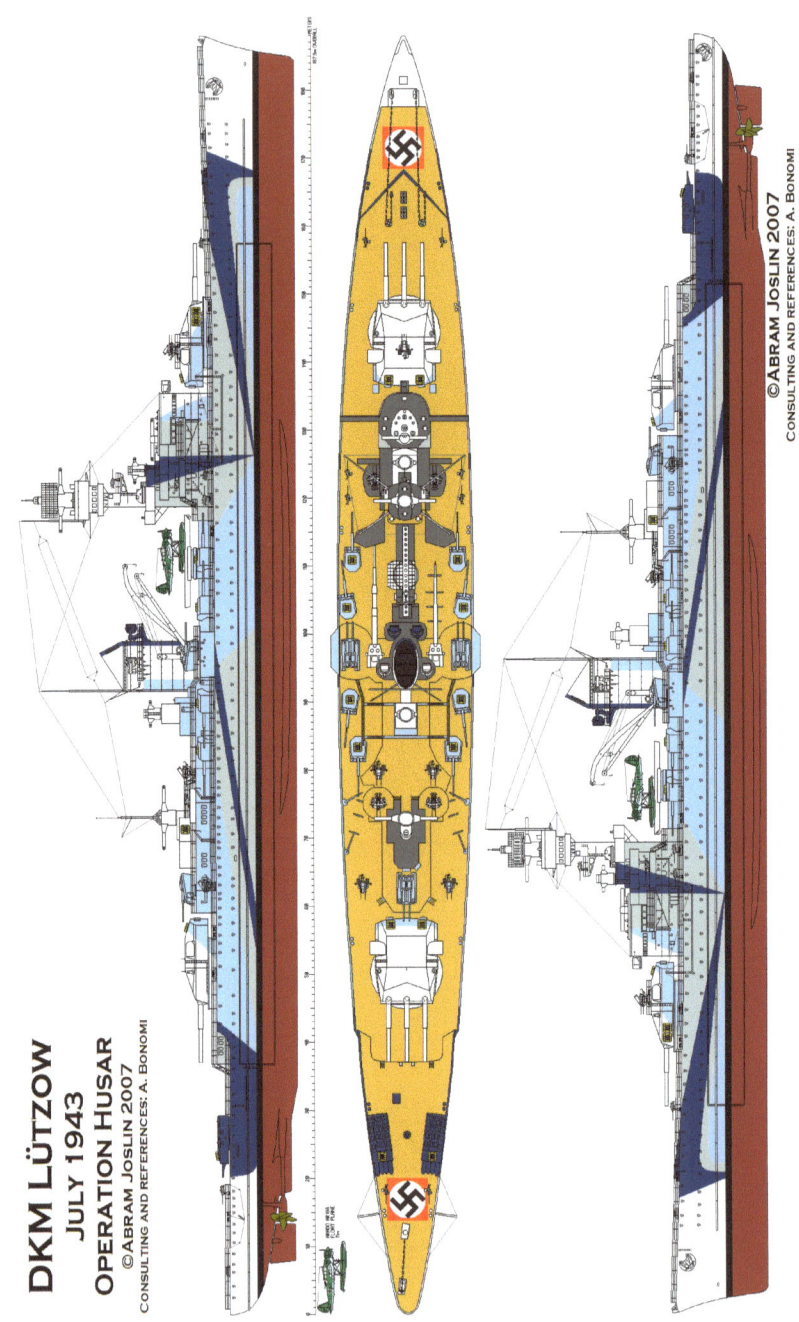

Figure 39. Profiles and plan for *Lutzow* with the Siberian camouflage for Operation *Husar* in July 1943. (Illustration by Abram Joslin)

Figure 40. *Lutzow* in the Baltic Sea in autumn 1943.

Figure 41. *Lutzow* enters Gotenhafen in June 1944.

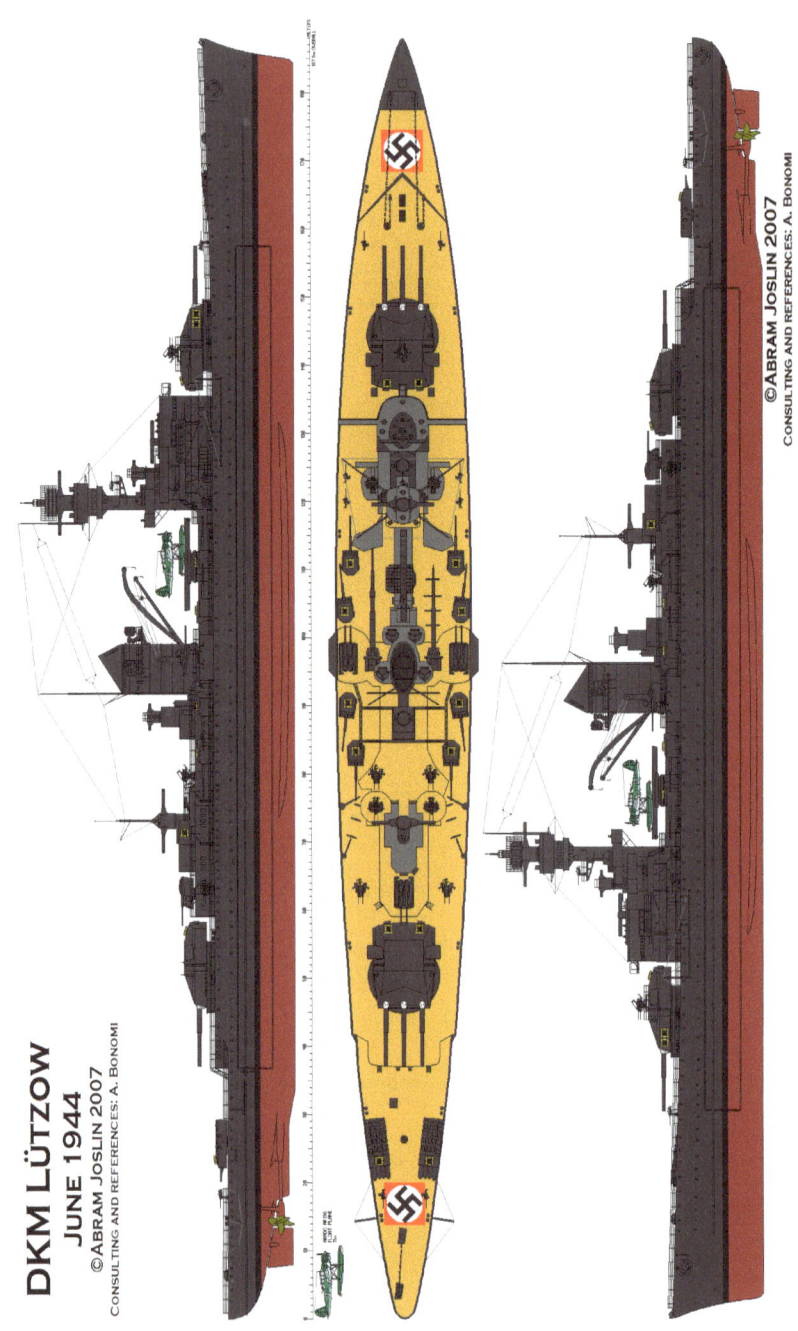

Figure 42. Profiles and plan for *Lutzow* in June 1944 with a dark camo scheme. (Illustration by Abram Joslin)

PANZERSCHIFFE DEUTSCHLAND (LUTZOW)

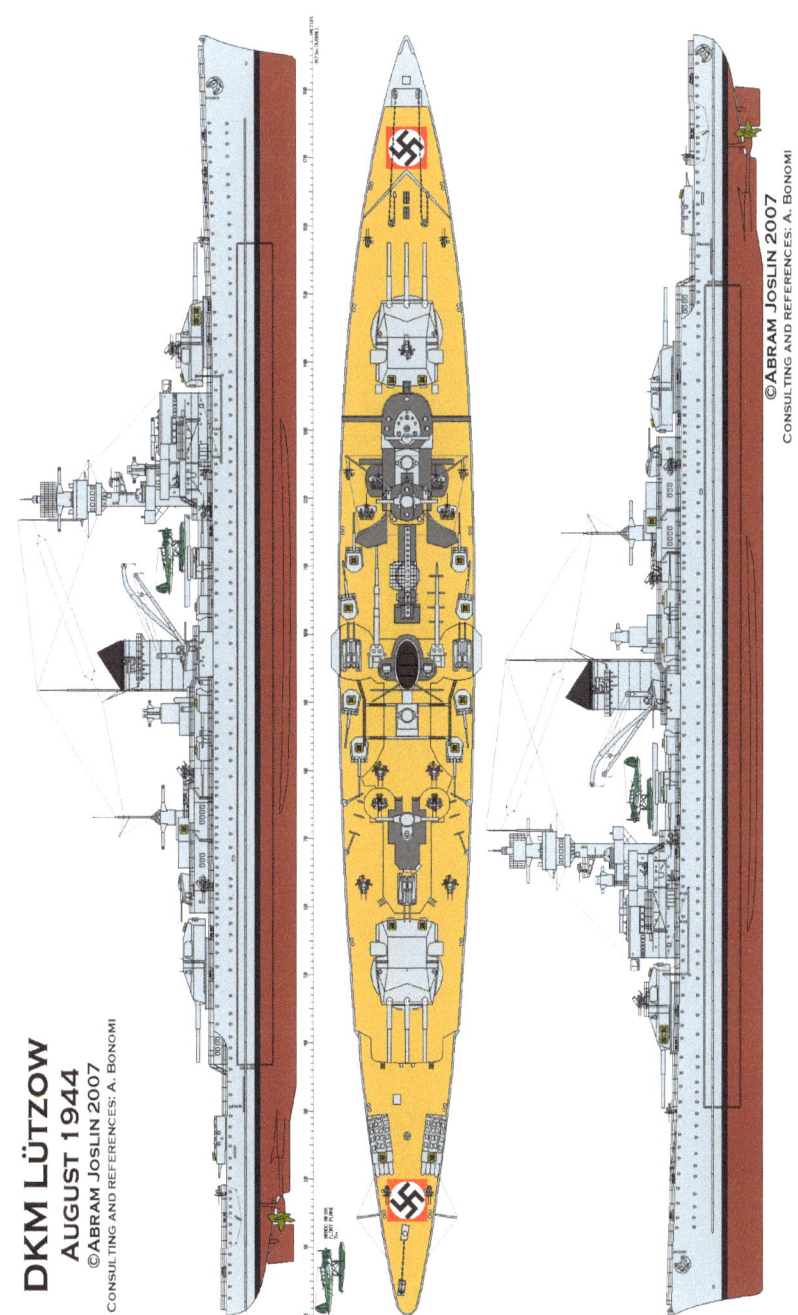

Figure 43. Profiles and plan for *Lutzow* with the new A/A guns—40 mm Bofors and twin 37 mm cannon—plus a new radar set in August 1944. (Illustration by Abram Joslin)

Figure 44. *Lutzow* at Swinemunde in summer 1944.

Figure 45. *Lutzow* anchored at Gotenhafen harbour at Seebanhof in late 1944.

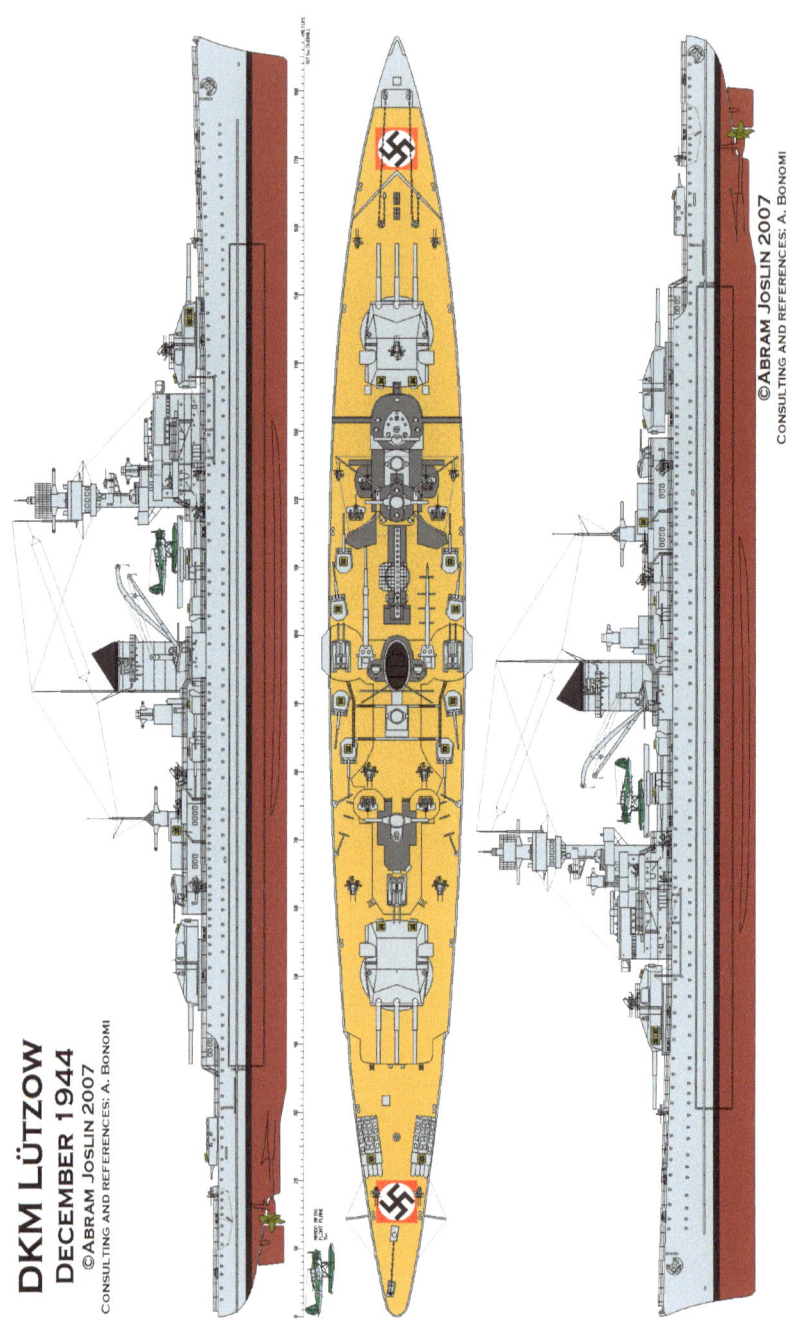

Figure 46. Profiles and plan, December 1944, for *Lutzow* with new additional 40 mm Bofors and 37 mm twin A/A sets. (Illustration by Abram Joslin)

PANZERSCHIFFE DEUTSCHLAND (LUTZOW)

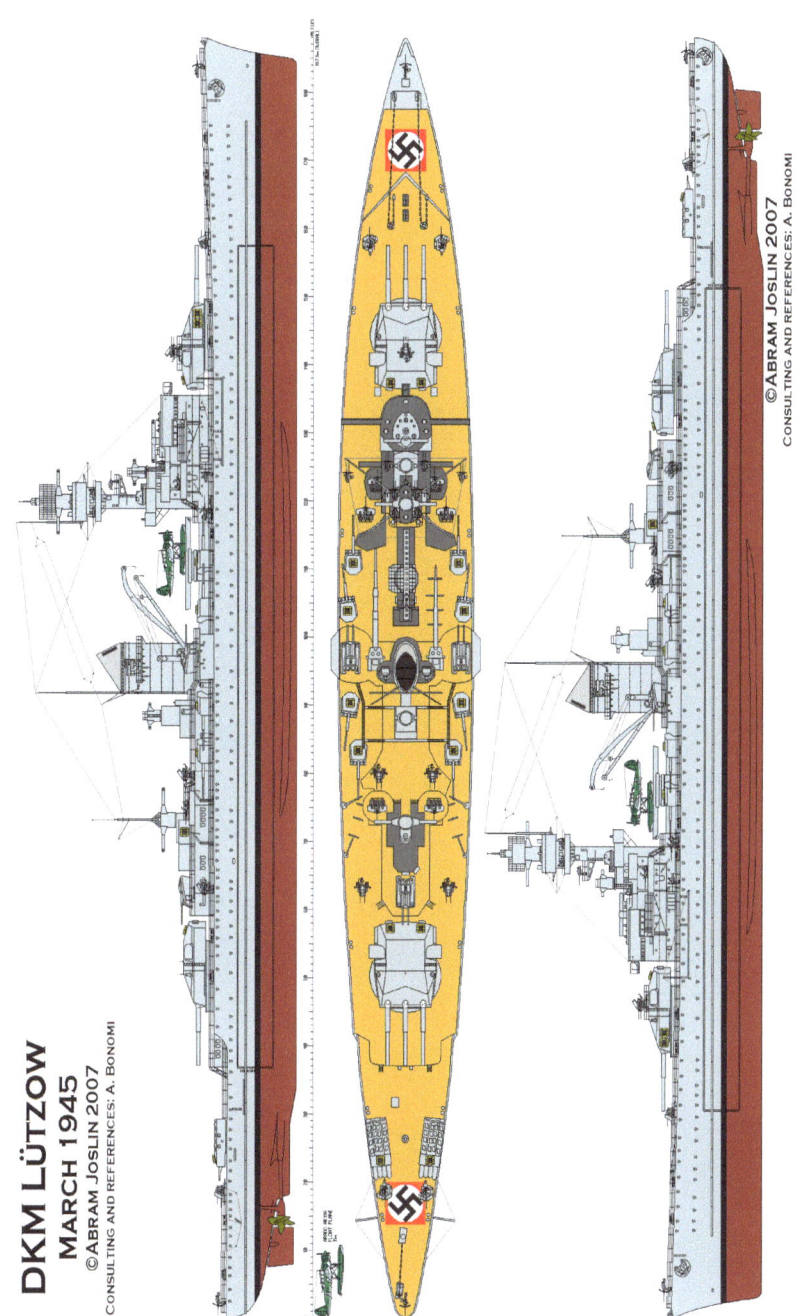

Figure 47. Profiles and plan, March 1945. *Lutzow* has latest A/A configuration including new 37 mm vertical twin shielded sets (Illustration by Abram Joslin)

Figure 48. *Lutzow* in early 1945 in the Baltic Sea; notice the shielded A/A guns.

Panzerschiffe Deutschland (Lutzow)

Figure 49. A Tallboy bomb of 5.2 tons especially designed to sink the *Tirpitz* by E. Wallis.

Figure 50. R.A.F. bomber Avro Lancaster releasing a Tallboy bomb.

Figure 51. *Lutzow* at Swinemunde after the Lancaster attack with Tallboys. Notice the huge bomb crater aside the ship.

PANZERSCHIFFE DEUTSCHLAND (LUTZOW)

Figure 52. *Lutzow* after being scuttled by her own crew on May 1945 at Swinemunde.

NIMBLE BOOKS LLC

Figure 53. *Lutzow* sinks below the waves for good on August 22, 1947

www.ingramcontent.com/pod-product-compliance
Lightning Source LLC
Chambersburg PA
CBHW040055160426
43192CB00002B/79